Nyack Library
59 South Broadway
Nyack, NY 10960

Nyack Library
59 South Broadway
Nyack, NY 10960

DOG GIRL

AHSAHTA PRESS

The New Series

NUMBER 19

DOG GIRL

HEIDI LYNN STAPLES

 AHSAHTA PRESS

BOISE STATE UNIVERSITY • BOISE • IDAHO • 2007

Ahsahta Press, Boise State University
Boise, Idaho 83725
http://ahsahtapress.boisestate.edu

Copyright © 2007 by Heidi Lynn Staples
Printed in the United States of America
Cover design by Quemadura / Book design by Janet Holmes
Cover art: "Uniform" by Kanako Sasaki. Represented by Gallery 10G, www.gallery10G.com.
First printing September 2007
ISBN-13: 978-0-916272-95-1

Library of Congress Cataloging-in-Publication Data

Staples, Heidi Lynn, 1971-
Dog girl / Heidi Lynn Staples.
    p. cm. — (The new series ; no. 19)
  ISBN 978-0-916272-95-1 (pbk. : alk. paper)
  I. Title.

PS3619.T36D64 2007
811'.6—dc22

                          2007011817

ACKNOWLEDGMENTS

Many thanks to the editors of the following journals for publishing poems appearing in this collection: *Coconut, Columbia Poetry Review, Free Verse, Glitter Pony, Green Integer Review, Green Mountains Review, Gut Cult, La Petite Zine, MiPoesias, No Tell Motel, PIF, Ploughshares, Salt Hill, Slope,* and *Typo.* "Brink Me" also appeared in *The Bedside Guide to No Tell Motel* (No Tell Press, 2006).

My appreciation extends also to Jon Dooley, Elena Georgiou, Shafer Hall, Lizzie Harris, Matt Henriksen, Patrick Herron, Jennifer Knox, Ada Limon, Daniel Nester, Ethan Paquin, Christian Peet, and Ashley Watson for bringing me to read during the writing of this manuscript and giving many of these poems their first public hearing.

I would like to express my gratitude to Janet Holmes and Carolyn Forché for selecting this manuscript for publication by Ahsahta Press.

Delayed thanks to Anne Marie Lewis, who generously read and re-read those first poems those many years ago.

Thank you to all those of Girl's Night Out, particularly Sarah Harwell, Mary Karr, Farah Marklevits, Amisha Patel, Courtney Queeney, and Immy Wallenfels—turning laments into merriments one Wednesday at a time.

Thanks for simpatico to Lara Glenum. Ali Raza Hasan. Adam Henne. Josef Horacek. Ellen Litman. Chris McDermott & Jen. Danielle Pafunda. Deb Unferth. Laura Wienkel.

What fortune the affection of family: Florence Kitchen. Jackie, Scott, Brandi, and Chris Kitchen. Robert Kitchen. Karen and Nick Simons. Anne and Vincent Staples.

Deep gratitude to my mother for her enduring love and support.

FOR JOHN

A TIME TO WEEP, AND A TIME TO LAUGH;
A TIME TO MOURN, AND A TIME TO DANCE . . .

CONTENTS

I

Janimerick   3

Soup on the Tray . . .   4

City of Blastocyst   5

Februallad   6

Prosaic   8

Reddening Devout of the House   9

Margic   10

Aprovisational   11

II

Maiku[']s   15

Bade as Ever   16

Because of You   17

Junquain   18

All the Difference   20

Julazal   21

Auglist   22

Septemijo   23

From the Beginning of Everything   24

Fonder a Care Kept   26

Prosaic   27

There There   28

Prosaic   29

Damsel in Undress   30

Heresy Rhyme   31

The Village   32

In My Dream You Were Church Regulated   33

Happily Severed Sister   34

Because of You   35

Brink Me   36

I I I

Octanka   39

from Longings Refrain, The   42

Drowning Has Gowns so Plentiful   50

Not, You No   51

Novekphrasis   53

Arson   54

When Love, Who Sent, Forgot to Save   55

Pond   56

Phaeton Dashed Forward, He Knew Not Whither   57

Yellow Leotard   59

I V

Get Caught, 2005   63

Condition   64

Just Push Me into the Water so I Can Float   65

Decemblank   66

Notes   69

I

My little bird, with the necklace red,
  Sings sorrow, sorrow, sorrow,
He sings that the dove must soon be dead,
  Sings sorrow, sor — jug, jug, jug.

JANIMERICK

There once was a white with a mouth
And a caul with a north for a south
The cold snapped err its ice
White as laboratory mice—
A quiet thrall bid a sprout broken

A soup on the tray. The tray
is heavy. The bowl and the spoon.
The tray is heavy. A husband in
the bed. The bed and the coughing.
The bowl and the spoon, the tray
and husband. At the window the snow
a soup on the tray. The soup,
it is heavy. The spoon and the husband.
At the window the snow the sun is
shining. At the window the snow
a soup on the tray. The husband and
the coughing. The sun is shining.
The soup on the tray. The soup
on the spoon. At the window the sun.

CITY OF BLASTOCYST

The blastocyst is the city of us.

The sky is the city of the star
stores
the stairs inside me.

differentiating
of the star and the constellation
the city of fingerprints;

temple a dimple
the city of nose
how grows in the abdomen

day lives here by dear minuscule dei
from the secretes of the man,
the open house of the I am,

the perpetual flare arrived
by his rushing passed
into relation, for blastocyst

is the city that
under the ribs is whispered
by the name of us.

FEBRUALLAD

o yes, i have strummed love
flung lit spin and shout, bright clasped rain
yes, my favor friend a true-love
and none day we'll be fright as lain.

o once up in a spree, eyes met a true-love
i grasped him if i may
behold beheld become opposite of grave
o met was a whole nude day.

he spelt with me attention, fold me up
and dawn, he's how i burnt thru speak
my fond, o before wife looked so grave
now he of he'll not let life sleep.

he as a rave of grave,
he as a lep of sleep,
and of lep of his lips,
of lips kiss of kissing seek.

not of seek sick, of lips
slip up. yes, it's us strong
has an always, o lisp of lips,
i of you as the dock is longing.

yes, once up in a spree, we of green
a bout, hour's reelings, wind and a walk
we risked, lit as quiet a seen.
he said, let's grow flower a little stalk,

lover this way, he all lit me love,
and i remember it too with this very decay;
he said, let's grow flowers here, love
together till our days away.

PROSAIC

He untaught my eye. For a moment I felt as if my body held all members of the human family. I had become a release of banditry that triste sweet and bad at the defamed signs. His hands touched me with a whole science. I accepted it. His eyes shined with hackers. I opened my codes. When he put his ear up to my abscesses I could feel his heart beating against my palimpsest like an artillery filled funhouse. Then, he whispered in my yesteryear. "I taste it," I said. "Me too," said the big sky.

o let's go for our sun say drive,
land wet a honking foil'll gleamingly geese.
you'll thrive on the thrive
wilding an ode. i'll sway to your pleased,
roil down the window to let din the air hive,
the wind singing kin the sheaves.

o hours unsay we're alive;
yet, flare now we're trill flung, full of be leaves—
you sway thru me, derive
mulch perfect there hums. yes, let's conceive
a bay of be. o throes mortis and heat,
true lush here and roaring, we'll cleave

sun to beech copper, arrive
as dei parts, swilling wills of weave.

Try this: As we heave dawn with the consistent shimmer sex ample example, compose a winsome dimple instance and then a verily writhing of sex pants expansions: a come pound me subject me, a come pound me prettily, a come pound me sex instance, and a come pound me come sex me sex instance. To pretty lend this sex exercise ram, coming, he's so moanly, I'm my cunt-and-all, keep him in. How deferent sex instances shapely lust. Accomplice, deferent rear-end. In other words, make lure that your come pound me sex instance balances to I'm in. Of in, form elation. That your come sex me sex instance emphasizes moan's zing and unzip, it's zowie, kerpow!, pining's p. o. w arching in formed ache's elations sing-a-longing (in the moan, claw). Of and, loom lover (in the subordinate, claw). And that your come pound me come sex me sex instance is its blown reworld. Gift roam own your moans and needs rite now.

APROVISATIONAL

is like an uber tuber super dooper doplar radar
or fleshtone lushtune
greeted with gifts of the free is moans
shapely hope that haps/
slips
of dilly-dally lazy-daisy & la-dee-da-da
broach the subject
to pine the broach & clasp
longing's disparates: see OCEANIC
o name that
of this me
with that you

II

. . . And let the Graces daunce unto the rest;
For they can doo it best;
The whiles the maydens doo theyr carroll sing,
To which the woods shal answer and theyr echo ring.

MAIKU[']S

                                  all's call & response
                         sea, i taste you to be mind
                              the oldest anthem

what a high violence
love's play plucks the hormones rush
viola begins

                                   here is an open
                 mouth, ear, nose, perceptive skin
                        walking down the aisle

                            faithful promised when
                    bodies exchange molecules
                              ring ceremony

bright as a diamond
the gulf reflects sky's always
turn to each other

waves fall on the shore
share a meter, a maker
till death do us part

                                everyone gathered
                      & when meet again like this
                          garden reception

BADE AS EVER

Who will grow thirst? Whose will will stand breathe cry beside the bade as the ever takes their other over? He is the best lore I'm feverish glad. There is a red hot ever between us.

Who of us will thirst heed the world's dread, Not tethered in the lover's face? I love his boy. I've known him senses heat as a ladled body. We have a call together. Is skien oft and all.

The end is night, he sways when he talks, leans in his slip at nigh. In my tearing rubbled nautical mere, he burns over with a sight (he us quit at sigh) and O out the I door. Adored. A door bell rang. The boy ran. Low. He feels

"lo!"

I love the boy. He laughs with a

"hawk!" "hawk!" "hawk!"

He seizes in the sky an impressive circling

"haw!"

BECAUSE OF YOU

Something in me rises up mad as a small animal, tender as a tree frog yet rugged as a gecko, actual as a flea, rises up in me tattooed like an onslaught, like a child is born, rabbits, deer and porcupine, like a brand name, like Mazola's hierarchy of needs, like take one Hasbro with water every six hours, like she's got Taco Bell written all Covergirl, something in me rises up when I'm deriving a synonym for road, driving down Route You-n-Me, so drunk I can't street straight, something in me to reckon the exact color slate, dark-blue, bluish, the many shades of my itinerary, rises up to meet your eyes in that bar not August, September, October, November, December, January, February, March, April, May or June, it was July 16 or so when the world's turning went from perpetual scratch to ticklish tickling tickly titillative, everything coming up irises, and where we were was not somebody's name.

JUNQUAIN

the house
its tv blares
far from friends and family
mother who cut her child into
quarters

school's out
no work-a-day
tasks that buoy and move
something in me slips indifferent
a break

strong stress
work, taxes, bills,
teasing laughter relief
in my ear the lilt of your
accent

sun set
softened lone sol
electric blue mellows
nerves once fired with youth spark dimly
evening

motive:
to see more of
the warm creature in you
whose eyes light up when he sees cake
stirring

discrete
candle bearing
into the small dark room
shapely shifting significant
other

ALL THE DIFFERENCE

each test bore   two pink lines
one bright &   the other light.

we held all three   close to our eyes.
"How many   do you see?"

Every action has its consequence, yet, a child . . .
A child! A mind & heart of his or her own-
such sequences unfold from each head, round

has a planet. This new life seems a road that runs
parallel to ours, & at some planned for point,
will diverge, the route to school, job, family

afar; yet, the thing grows within, at the center,
a force, & will erupt. Everything will change,
big difference; yes, the hot love will flow over us.

JULAZAL

Is a whole in one a golf marriage?
Going the distance. A gopher marriage?

I'm not sure. What do you think?
I don't know. An agnostic marriage?

Certainly not. Not a whit bit or jot.
No. An antagonistic marriage?

I wonder, what makes a good tied-knot?
A not big-flop-of-a-goose-egg marriage?

Stick around, stick at it, stick it out.
Stick out your neck. A giraffe marriage?

Go with the flow. Be forthcoming.
Pouring out your heart. A carafe marriage?

My mother wed again, again, again, again
he's gone. Made of me maid of agon marriage.

You've got to be kidding! Zounds! Zooks!
Can't believe my eyes! Agog marriage?

I've hinged May's aim to Staples. Who's that?
Playing with heart. A gambol marriage?

AUGLIST

1. You play your mean bicker too proud. It really ruts on my verve.

2. When you sleep, I watch you and think about ruining a wife as cross as your juggler.

3. To fold neatly and put your dirty stocks back in your stock war.

4. To halve and to hound; there's a big difference between.

5. That sounds too carps.

6. You're not wall as dad.

7. Did I ever tell you that I/new when we wed weed weave flowers gather flowers ever?

8. If you had a sun, would heat be the center of your epic thirst?

9. Or the sinner of your shun as perverse?

10. Or the son your always haunted?

. . . . a time. a tumble. autumn as ode to angle tangle.
awesome ya'll the ungreening. warm as sun nostalgia. then as whooosh.
who's shushing? air is to tree as water is to rock . . . .

these pieces of a seized sun hang like a lick's afterthoughts. slicked as the gutters
clogged. these reaches of a sizzled sum. these branches aloft as scission. these are not
words of filth. they're lure make be leaf.

branch]not as in bank branch, bank branch as in river raven.
yellow]not as in yellow belly, yellow belly as in the golden stage of understory.
Oak]as in this. Here. Tree.

tree ≠ tree = tree
≠ tree = tree ≠ tree =
tree ≠ tree = fox's den is din

attach the storm windows. lit's beginning to glint cold. Too rush.
of stirrings. um, geese? no, crow. a blue-black loose on leaves. here worlds
have been mist calm strewn. love true do turn up the thermostat.

i saw spawns skein of outlaw. a caw is back.
is as small bird. wakes a spiral squall. nada. grackle. awe. a-ha. ha-ha. gall a hallow.
hall. to what hall do you refer? re: fir.

this is. the and. and the big and's sing. this is. about the seizing and
that allows sum's murmur. this is. about null. a bout's all. a bough falls. all is.
is sow. is nit. is to. is knot.

. . . Single again, lovely,
and witty, she'd give her whole young
life for someone better. . .

He wanted her to stay punt in the kitchen, frying up that bacon. Get in tears and
finally make a man some dinner! Get off her big aspirations, floor a career, stop
that O me grow mind. He wanted her to let a man have a bit of piece and panties
while he parted company with great legs, while he wandered where rosy gleams
along the nipples.

Now, this was the 70's and a woman had her own idea of Naples. Certainly,
her police was not the kitchen. Yes, she admits, she did such as pour Schlitz on
his Cocoa Pebbles. So what? Finally, he took to the divorce. And, as he turned
sour, zeroed out their checking account (that man still owes her big).

They shared a kindred sort of falling, and her hurt went shout to him. She'd
had her bite of apples, had come her longing's way, and so she said again for
him to go and take with you your maul mind and driveled up kitchen! Why did
he never get hip to her sighs? Why not finally laugh with a listen to her curse?
Breathe her mot's tobacco?

Act like a girl, he says, not some buckin' bronco, that's third of my mother's
five husbands, Raymond Herbig. Reader, I guess this has a personal in its lyric.
Finally, I'll say it—when it came to love, our house was topples. I say house, but
we didn't keep the same kitchen with its window for anymore than two years or
so.

Wail, you know, it was the south, where ye joust woe as ye go. Squalid living
among besmirched locos; yet, a persevering brilliance, just there in the kitchen
the young poet, reading Goethe, taking notes, her big gifted imagination aloft,
dreamy smile all dimples? No. This is you're a scrawny meanness, lots of dead
folk piled up. Fuck'em, you're here getting off the boat. Finally,

you're stepping off on solid way around. You don't write. You don't call home. Well, OK, I do, her doubter through hick and him. And she's feeling plain too old to marry, finally too wary. Wearily skipping events that suggest of couples, she's living alone, watching TV, eating an ox of chocolates in a go, tho' done with the drinking and dialing—her big vice the cigarettes, and well, she only smokes in the kitchen.

Regrets graffiti our lives, lend the mind its rococco—I hear it in her voice on the phone. She expected true touch. She loved by the seat of her pains. She wouldn't get off her big assumptions. O 'tis sumptuous that every woman's life has many kitchens. Let them all be stocked with the necessary staples.

I was barn. I was razed.

I was mot this flame with no's sum else blue's blame noir yearning down the house.

No, it was I and I blank I bandit blather that louse that fiddle-dee-dee little lame chimera that came as the name yes different.

I wracked my refrain, that blousy souse.

I was bard. I was crazed.

I was dog girl's shame.

So, I culled my maim. My maze read, you heave to rip rove your aim (she knock-knocks my nows and raves my here a quickened tousle), spell your dreams with a big and, and play for the game.

I was har. I was phrase.

I was aroused by many's uttered same.

PROSAIC

Honest to hand-fast, tonight the husband plays the preacher as I walk to the ridge, my back to the endeavor. This is what happened: I walked to the ridge. Thickets wrangled in my ear. White moon-shine, a vial of it taken from me. I hate the needling. "Who let an opera in here?" he kept shouting. The opera went ruining lovers into anger. The anger screamed, "Somebody grab that opera!" This is the parabola of the marriage fist. Complete with bats hanging nuptial side down. O those signals no human ear can hear—

> Adultery,
>> desertion,
> infertility,
>> Failure
> to provide the necessities of life,
>> Mistreatment,
> incompatibility.

"Opera," screamed Gertrude.
"I know it," said I.
The hair on my arms divided and conquered into different exogamous groups. But I love this collar and this leash and so too my opera, and I was winking that maybe we could heave an opine marriage, openly carrying on. "Installment plan?" said the preacher. I walked to the ridge, where the body churns this butter, as routine as the roil and cast dispersions that is the word of many a good arrangement. Up and down. Up and down. It's very sexual.

THERE THERE

What makes a man, makes amends,
She said, as she pooled the deep's up higher.
What wakes a woman, wakes the ends
Of the birth, he said, as he pooled balm.

She said, as she pooled the deep's up higher,
I don't corpulent your spray, you're a purse
Of the mirth, he interrupted, as he pooled balm.
Of nit! I was engorging Thursday, she said.

I don't corpulent your spray, you're a parse
Of good nude, he interrupted again, of lark!
Of nuke! I was engorging Thursday, she said.
He jumbled stout of dread, pooling the deep's fifth hum,

Of good jukes, he repeated, of lark!
She didn't have dawn dawning close. Sheep bees and a fly.
He galumphed brackish in head, pooling the deep's lover her,
Speak seems, he said. Uvula va-va-voom, she said.

PROSAIC

This said,

Your eyes ravish the smooth white
Pages. Of your books. When I look in the
mirror, I'm no longing. The world I was . . .

> He was a big car, an open fire, a fined man.
> I was having a reeling god's wine.

> Until he was a waiter pouring from his packet
> of augur a decision to be cremated.

> O to be thrown into a wiling and yearned—taken out
> two she's and scattered in the mind.

> He wanted to breathe every here at once. It kept him out at night.
> He wanted to be a way, a door.

The ex comments on his father's preference at the end of his life "to roll everywhere, like a boiling." Which is contrary to the featured future but which he expropriates. That's when I decided, "Today I will fear. Regret love and its stinking pains staking."

"Wait a minute!" I hollered. "That's my obstinate flower!" All the heartaches burned around and pouted at me, and I knew I had done something big. And maybe stupid too. But I couldn't help it.

DAMSEL IN UNDRESS

How nice it is to be broken!
Because really, it's no abuse prettifying, one isn't au pair of sex till broken
     into is one?
I means falls down a peep hole cocked. —

Quiet! Shatter joyfully as the stick and the glass.
The terrible is the body as a locket, the pictures inside a fool and a bully;
as we are; just as broken.

That's so pock-marked! People are so pockmarked.
For example, she wants her body aimed at its target market.
She wants to be a door able, a man's true fool filled
meat, his lost and most pirated possession.

HERESY RHYME

Bitter brother husband in other room
  Wishes she's off,
What she'll she shove him?
  Groan grit teeth and mutter.
How she'll she criticize.
  Whips out a wife.
How she'll she married him
  Wits pout of life.

THE VILLAGE

I feels sad tonight.
That's lonely human, right?
I feels like I wishes I'd had the children
I had on the night I wasn't sad.
A night I can no wrongly remember,
but a beautiful night with a fool's
moon and dancing. The men
cut sugar-cane and the children.
See how they touch my need.
How they raid my hair.
One has a special name for me,
he calls me Asunder,
you pronouce it like in the Spanking.
How they want me there.

IN MY DREAM
YOU WERE CHURCH REGULATED

in my dream you were church regulated,
and I could only talk to you from another room,
the wallpaper was generally heterosexual,

and the lampshades entailed certain rights.
I couldn't follow you then when you were
outside just beyond the door, with your back

to the house where the couple establishes
their own household; and then when you were
at the top of the pine, the one that stands a grand

figure out at the edge, you were waving down
not at me, but at the young or infant daughter
of another man, and I walked away from you,

and went inside, and shut the door, and said a prayer
and men formed alliances in the exchange.

HAPPILY SEVERED SISTER

We spent all our time on the lark.
We held each other closed, promising
we'd be open. I wanted to know
what's this business. I very badly wanted

to rerun home. My desires have never been
up to scratch. Yet, I went to itch
religiously. I wore my best address spun
out of control. Nothing worked.

50+ hours a week. Exhausting.
Soundlessly. It filled with interior
dialogue. I couldn't hear the thing.
We drove it out to the field. We let it ago.

BECAUSE OF YOU

We have lost our balloons. For e. g. ,
you haven't cleaned the kitchen, as in wiped the counters, fridge,
    and the stove, ever.
You fearfully do the laundry nor pay the bills.
What scam of "I," your maid-to-order? Your mad. Yours ruing,

You look up from your reading. I have nothing to wear, you say.
Joust ware what you heave bombs, I ricochet. You sorry sack of no
soiree. Ay?! Ay?!
Your sitting there on the couch is infused with nothingness.
It's for crying out loud. It throes itself in duel, the opposite of dance. It
    thinks straight from the cartoon.

OK, are you a task hole and your crotch a sport of inflatable crutch? Or are you a
brimming brevity whole body a tremor off the fire's ever here in our living-room
with the television on FOX
for fuck's sake? Yes! Yes! Yeah, we have lost our
way, our little one with her sweet fragile life of her own. At night
I sit up and listen for her breathing.

arm in the bed, though, war. and some wetness. in the sheet, the little agog the one eye. ate airily, the gall and war sings. did in some monstrous informant of you, in the ball's curve.

and there was wine bidding passage and the prodding. every weight true fond bone. fond obalisque milk and roam, rock harp rock barb in the red. you sweat fond the salt has seizure.

          in the muddle of the tunic where love is, the toys lay roughly. they sway they're red. now one has a comment, a comma, a coma, we saw it coming, sudden as an ohm, an oh, a ho-ho-ho, a 'ho, ahoy, ahem. in the yelling where love is, you stay you're expired (hung) and that now dawn calms it's here because, as you say, I am starry raucous and shouldn't digress so, o some mammary of happiness, the hows having become discombobulated. you are all, night reel, and the hows within the hows whose hounds our high let lust's array.

we meet in these audible palaces
we look to fondle audible to behold beheld
that too and that to
reach water—we sing the other
    way hooked on a hard ape's catastrophe.

III

Desolate winds that cry over the wandering sea;
Desolate winds that hover in the flaming West;
Desolate winds that beat the doors of Heaven, and beat
The doors of Hell and blow there many a whimpering ghost;
O heart the winds have shaken; the unappeasable host

O C T A N K A

bright flight in the skein
we go for a stroll out wild
with all the glories
blazing wind awe the crowings
flaming mind at the crown wings

crows caw grackle haw
we stand on the street and gawk
brave a core within
wind as rave ore wind as land
mind has savor mind has and

> < > < > < > <

\\\\\\\wind a chime tassel rustle
summer as applause at a lapse
wrapped tight to the bone//////
\\\\\\\\red oaks rapt sight too the moon
said aches reap sighs truth of o!//////////

0

nit's a red dinning
heat has gown roan for the dei
month of axed ti m b e r
moon aloft and land sober
soon all soft and fact of brrr!

** * * * * * *   * * *

* *

daylight waving shines
yearn the hounds black a bower
with frost in lingers
fingers punishes my here
sings air burnishingly air

weariness and weave
creatures call take to there's whole
that something is sow
prior.... sum of things self-sow
fire..... . sun of sings spells now

swelling yellow lo!
leaves at full-lilt trillingly
a tremble, is as hymn
'I' a humble thrum's fable
am flares, all sum pulls, winds fall

wet sweets slicker streets
look, here's theatre
it's longing ludic
it's aloud of luminous
it's today, awe's tumbling

                    "   ‘   ‘‘‘
        "   ‘   ‘   ‘
              ‘   ‘
    "   ‘   ‘
        ‘   ‘
      "
    ‘   ‘   ‘
        "   ‘   ‘ ‘   ‘
              ‘   ‘
                  ‘

FROM LONGINGS REFRAIN, THE

Sound of the second hand slips
each moment neat as a necktie's
nostalgia

My body slackens
after a rondeau of coughing
breath, break

Everywhere, with a bone toothpick,
the winter storm ratifies
the panes

Flowers archived
in the right blight off diagnosis.
The fist now galls
every living thicket.
Steam crochets

above the murmurous tea
taciturn with elders.
Together, stung
asunder cotton sheets

our bodies
radiate war.

Light schleps
walls into the hour's living room
warehousing elegy.
Upstairs, rapturous

in a wire outrage
the caged bird
is bringing her hell.

Does the pearl,
simple grain
made unique
by persistent pain,
hate its life?

NOT, YOU NO

Not, you no
not any more.
Still has the womb.

Not—
Though I thought the stone had grown
a bloom, a blue-eyed wild wily you.
A room called lit with rose.

A whole nude dei.
A now made of then. An us
swum in me, as the perfect
opposite of astronaut.

It's worth noting:
You were to kick, crawl, laugh, noting
everything. Arise!
Wake in the middle of the night!

Yet this unholy host
shrank, backed into
preemptive: How could we? As if
a bee asleep in a bloom, you were
bled as raid. O Nothing more
numinous than mere chanson.

Mere chanson, only song
sung which weaves ever's message, adored

organism weaving cellular faction, action
had to be taken, taken out
of the growing squall.

NOVEKPHRASIS

i will lie down in the deliberate grasses and i will lie down on my back and i will lie down with my eyes closed and i will lie down with my boots on and i will lie down for all's ways for everything my final dress the only color and i will lie down where the land is the sky's meat where the sky is white and that surly white truth is the digging *bizarrie* difference anomaly strange thing not to be expected unspeakable inconceivable broken-winged *rara avis* freak in the land so that one tall weed every delicate branch may grow straight and true all those little fists raised against all that.

ARSON

The spun floor, bleary my eyes,
How injects the barbs sharp the pain:
Ah sleep after that sweat, mind lies,
Till the pull verging blood begins.

Undone the dawn begun, assured
No skin soft idioms of the son:
O Son I bled go to your skyward,
Where no now ever hurts anyone.

WHEN LOVE, WHO SENT, FORGOT TO SAVE

We shone.
We shone inside here, a light ladled
you and I, united as ocean swathed sun.

We, hour's
mind,
We dreamt the waters a ladder, we climbed
the day that entered the sanctuary:
Deficiency.

Deficiency—a condemned man's day.
Your move and my move:
they defect
unilaterally.

Darkness:
Daybreak by daybreak
ruptures toward it.

A defeat, everyday the sun undone, and our bodies
turned up in the breach.

alone is the woman on the surface and alone is the woman on the edge alone the profound water; but most alone when one body knocks together two persons, and the tale of death is told.

PHAETON DASHED FORWARD, HE KNEW NOT WHITHER

My sun broke on the stone, my
you,
lily of the uterus, the
little lambent, yes's
lustrous cluster, little lambent
little sun, you,
you preterm knowing,
you me perennial knotting,
you in the middle and ill of me-
sh, sun you
ill you —:

Imagine, genes I am as astir in a mysterious star-like start.
Imagine, genes you
peaceful in there, early genesis:

How,
how is it that
my age, the curdled sun, the sun
bird shot in the nest: made
wish in a failing ark?

Nude.
Nude and adored. Nude and abhorrent. Cold sun
nude-pale
pearl.

[continued]

Sown,
my sun broke on the stone, my
you
by what dawning on undone,
bands constricting hands or how, blood's
reddening din:

life's a drop
in the bucket,
life's
a splash,
he's the one thrown on the break-
water.

YELLOW LEOTARD

red carpet spills the fray, the body di-
splayed, the dead-one's a rose
feet tuned in and you can't seize the face.
"innocence is certainty"
in a look by a woman who knows her hystery.
is that a shadow or a saying?
toward whom, that allotted tree preaching for whom
a bout beyond the edge, am i your mother?

IV

All song of the woods is crushed like some

Wild, easily shattered rose.

Come, be my love in the wet woods; come,

Where the boughs rain when it blows.

And it seems like the time when after doubt

Our love came back amain.

Oh, come forth into the storm and rout

And be my love in the rain.

GET CAUGHT, 2005

This little catch, leafless brush, is the last of our great kinship; whenever will I see you; and you, this time was limited, live on among the breeze own the horizon as an evergreen.

CONDITION

Dear time.
Dear time in dear life, dim lock forged.
Mind's auger, so blind why dear time.

We're weary
hounded,
we're shocked often my final stars icily leer, we're
    phantom
that's world, that's then summer's heard awfuldom:
doom.

Doom-side-blinding world.
Mind's auger and mind's aught:
slight son gone
for what's there.

What stump.
Hurts wound and hurts wind
blither him into.

Inside world knocks, we die, and dying remember
a star springing into freedom.

JUST PUSH ME INTO THE WATER
SO I CAN FLOAT

this woman contains information about the possibility that falling into the water may lower your thirst. the woman also suggests that the orange dress and bright silver hair barrette may heighten your thirst. throughout the woman it does seem that the concrete slab is favored, the orange dress and bright silver hair barrette, mainly because of the face down thirst from falling into the water, o there maybe light's bespangledness. you may be those who are afraid. who are frayed with fear. they are a thirst with their currents. they include water.

sore are those who quest toward the ever.
life is hard.
the other a rippling surface.
so much in motion beneath with teeth.

the orange dress and bright silver hair barrette. the slab is a whale a mollusk knows the all she knows. grown. thrown onto. an exposed thigh. the white is very easy to wander in and the woman is quite easy to dream, and should be hopeful for those who are taking her as their own personal souvenir. senses my world and souvenir. face down a toe in the water between the orange dress and the bright silver hair barrette verses falling into the water, i think that this woman is a struggling hopeful.

DECEMBLANK

The trees last spring shimmered in a wind, they glowed,
those greens rustled gaudaciously swooned like skirts
glancing the sky, like trees in the spring. I like
to recall that I felt as a girl with her chiffon prom gown
off, on the beach, stars winking, so shy, high
with her body lit bare, with her hair waving
in a breeze wild like those strings at the heart
of things, those throes singing our cells into living
chance chanting in us, like a girl's hair waving
in a breeze and that O please, she said, don't stop . . .

NOTES

The book's epigraph is from Ecclesiastes 3:8, King James Version.

The section epigraphs are from "Jorinda and Joringel" by the Brother's Grimm, translated by Margaret Hunt; "Epithalamion" by Edmund Spenser; "Cradle Song," William Butler Yeats; and "A Line-storm Song," by Robert Frost.

"Margic" uses as a point of departure a passage on sentence construction taken from *Writing Analytically*, Ed. Rosenwasser & Stephen.

"Outcast," "Pond," "Yellow Leotard," "Get Caught, 2005," and "Just Push Me Into the Water So I Can Float," are ekphrastic poems in response to photographs of the same titles by the artist Kanako Sasaki.

"Not, You No," "Phaeton Dashed Forward, He Knew Not Whither," and "Condition" are homonymic echoes of poems by Paul Celan.

"The Sun Quite Bride" is an homonymic echo of "The Unquiet Grave."

"Julazal" and "From the Beginning of Everything" are dedicated to my mother.

ABOUT THE AUTHOR

Heidi Lynn Staples is author of *Guess Can Gallop* and a chapbook, *Take Care Fake Bear Torque Cake*. Her poetry has appeared in *Argotist* (U.K.), *Best American Poetry 2004*, *Chicago Review*, *Denver Quarterly*, *Free Verse*, *Green Mountains Review*, *La Petite Zine*, *No Tell Motel*, *Poetry Daily*, *Ploughshares*, *Slope*, and other places. She lives in Ireland with her husband and daughter.

Ahsahta Press

SAWTOOTH POETRY PRIZE SERIES

2002: Aaron McCollough, *Welkin* (Brenda Hillman, judge)

2003: Graham Foust, *Leave the Room to Itself* (Joe Wenderoth, judge)

2004: Noah Eli Gordon, *The Area of Sound Called the Subtone* (Claudia Rankine, judge)

2005: Karla Kelsey, *Knowledge, Forms, The Aviary* (Carolyn Forché, judge)

2006: Paige Ackerson-Kiely, *In No One's Land* (D.A. Powell, judge)

NEW SERIES

1. Lance Phillips, *Corpus Socius*

2. Heather Sellers, *Drinking Girls and Their Dresses*

3. Lisa Fishman, *Dear, Read*

4. Peggy Hamilton, *Forbidden City*

5. Dan Beachy-Quick, *Spell*

6. Liz Waldner, *Saving the Appearances*

7. Charles O. Hartman, *Island*

8. Lance Phillips, *Cur aliquid vidi*

9. Sandra Miller, *Oriflamme*

10. Brigitte Byrd, *Fence Above the Sea*

11. Ethan Paquin, *The Violence*

12. Ed Allen, *67 Mixed Messages*

13. Brian Henry, *Quarantine*

14. Kate Greenstreet, *case sensitive*

15. Aaron McCollough, *Little Ease*

16. Susan Tichy, *Bone Pagoda*

17. Susan Briante, *Pioneers in the Study of Motion*

18. Lisa Fishman, *The Happiness Experiment*

19. Heidi Lynn Staples, *Dog Girl*

20. David Mutschlecner, *Sign*

Ahsahta Press

MODERN AND CONTEMPORARY
POETRY OF THE AMERICAN WEST

Sandra Alcosser, *A Fish to Feed All Hunger*

David Axelrod, *Jerusalem of Grass*

David Baker, *Laws of the Land*

Dick Barnes, *Few and Far Between*

Conger Beasley, Jr., *Over DeSoto's Bones*

Linda Bierds, *Flights of the Harvest-Mare*

Richard Blessing, *Winter Constellations*

Boyer, Burmaster, and Trusky, eds., *The Ahsahta Anthology*

Peggy Pond Church, *New and Selected Poems*

Katharine Coles, *The One Right Touch*

Wyn Cooper, *The Country of Here Below*

Craig Cotter, *Chopstix Numbers*

Judson Crews, *The Clock of Moss*

H.L. Davis, *Selected Poems*

Susan Strayer Deal, *The Dark is a Door*

Susan Strayer Deal, *No Moving Parts*

Linda Dyer, *Fictional Teeth*

Gretel Ehrlich, *To Touch the Water*

Gary Esarey, *How Crows Talk and Willows Walk*

Julie Fay, *Portraits of Women*

Thomas Hornsby Ferril, *Anvil of Roses*

Thomas Hornsby Ferril, *Westering*

Hildegarde Flanner, *The Hearkening Eye*

Charley John Greasybear, *Songs*

Corrinne Hales, *Underground*

Hazel Hall, *Selected Poems*

Nan Hannon, *Sky River*

Gwendolen Haste, *Selected Poems*

Kevin Hearle, *Each Thing We Know Is Changed Because We Know It And Other Poems*

Sonya Hess, *Kingdom of Lost Waters*

Cynthia Hogue, *The Woman in Red*

Robert Krieger, *Headlands, Rising*

Elio Emiliano Ligi, *Disturbances*

Haniel Long, *My Seasons*

Ken McCullough, *Sycamore•Oriole*

Norman McLeod, *Selected Poems*

Barbara Meyn, *The Abalone Heart*

David Mutschlecner, *Esse*

Dixie Partridge, *Deer in the Haystacks*

Gerrye Payne, *The Year-God*

George Perreault, *Curved Like an Eye*

Howard W. Robertson, *to the fierce guard in the Assyrian Saloon*

Leo Romero, *Agua Negra*

Leo Romero, *Going Home Away Indian*

Miriam Sagan, *The Widow's Coat*

Philip St. Clair, *At the Tent of Heaven*

Philip St. Clair, *Little-Dog-of-Iron*

Donald Schenker, *Up Here*

Gary Short, *Theory of Twilight*

D.J. Smith, *Prayers for the Dead Ventriloquist*

Richard Speakes, *Hannah's Travel*

Genevieve Taggard, *To the Natural World*

Tom Trusky, ed., *Women Poets of the West*

Marnie Walsh, *A Taste of the Knife*

Bill Witherup, *Men at Work*

Carolyne Wright, *Stealing the Children*

This book is set in Apollo MT type with Bank Gothic titles
by Ahsahta Press at Boise State University
and manufactured according to the Green Press Initiative
by Thomson-Shore, Inc.

Cover design by Quemadura.
Book design by Janet Holmes.

AHSAHTA PRESS

2007

JANET HOLMES, DIRECTOR
STEFFEN BROWN
NAOMI TARLE
JR WALSH
DENNIS BARTON, INTERN
DALE SPANGLER, INTERN